Contents

General Knowledge

1) Derby won their first game of the 21st century, a 2-0 win thanks to a brace from Branko Strupar against which team on the 3rd of January 2000?

2) Which company was Derby's main shirt sponsor during the 2007/08 Premier League campaign?

3) Who was the club's top scorer in the 2017/18 Championship season with 21 goals?

4) Tom Huddlestone made his debut in 2003 in an opening day fixture against which team?

5) Which player became the first Austrian to represent the club when he signed in 2015?

6) Who became Derby's youngest ever goal scorer when he netted in an FA Cup victory over Tranmere in 2013 aged just 16 years and 5 months old?

7) Which side did Derby beat on aggregate to progress to the Championship Play Off Final of 2007?

8) Who scored the winner in that 2007 final against West Brom?

9) Tom Huddlestone made his debut in 2003 in an opening day fixture against which team?

10) Which squad number did Tom Ince wear during his time at the club?

11) Who did Robbie Savage replace as club captain in 2008?

12) Who scored a calamitous own goal late on to hand Middlesbrough a 1-1 draw at the Riverside in October 2018?

13) England beat which county 4-0 at Pride Park in May 2001?

14) Who scored a hat trick in the 4-2 win over Fulham in April 2017?

15) Ashley Cole made his final appearance as a professional in a match versus which team in April 2019?

16) Who scored the winner as Derby won their only game of the 2007/08 Premier League season against Newcastle?

17) Which other two teams were relegated alongside Derby in the 2001/02 Premiership season?

18) Derby lost 1-0 to QPR in the 2014 Championship Play Off final despite which opposition player being dismissed with the score at 0-0?

19) By what aggregate score line did Derby defeat Leeds in their dramatic Play Off Semi Final tie in 2019?

20) Derby escaped relegation on the last day of the 2020/21 Championship season by drawing with Sheffield Wednesday, but what was the final score?

Transfers Part One

1) From which side did Derby buy Georgi Kinkladze in April 2000?

2) Who was sold to Lens in June 2000?

3) Which player was bought from Manchester United in July 2000?

4) Dean Sturridge left to join which side in January 2001?

5) Derby signed which two players from Newcastle United in February 2002?

6) Which midfielder was sold to Leeds United in October 2001?

7) Derby sold which two players to Middlesbrough in January 2003?

8) From which club was Paul Peschisolido signed in 2004?

9) Fabrizio Ravanelli joined which Scottish side on a free transfer after leaving in 2003?

10) Inigo Idiakez signed on a free from which Spanish club in the summer of 2004?

11) Which centre back joined from West Brom in January 2006?

12) Tom Huddlestone was sold to which Premier League team in 2005?

13) From which club did Derby buy Robert Earnshaw in 2007?

14) Goalkeeper Roy Carroll signed on a free from which club in January 2008?

15) Which winger arrived from Spanish side Levante in the 2008 January transfer window?

16) Which defender signed on a free in November 2008 having left Southampton?

17) Who was sold to Hull City in July 2008?

18) Derby signed which two players from Burton in July 2009?

19) Which England international midfielder joined from Sheffield United in September 2009?

20) Claude Davis joined which club after leaving Derby in September 2009?

Cup Games

1) Who scored the winner in the 1-0 victory over Crystal Palace in the FA Cup Third Round in January 2020?

2) What was the final score in the incredible penalty shoot-out win over Carlisle in the League Cup Second Round win in 2016?

3) Which non-league team knocked Derby out of the FA Cup in January 2011?

4) Which team knocked The Rams out of the league cup in both 2000 and 2001?

5) Derby lost 3-1 at home to which team in the 2014 League Cup Quarter Final?

6) By what score were Nottingham Forest beaten in the 2009 FA Cup Fourth Round replay at the City Ground?

7) Derby smashed which team 5-0 in the 2013 League Cup Second Round?

8) Derby also won 5-0 in the FA Cup in 2013, defeating which side?

9) Which five teams did Derby knock out on their way to the Semi Final of the 2008/09 League Cup?

10) Derby won the first leg of the 2009 Semi Final, beating Manchester United 1-0 thanks to a goal from which player?

Memorable Games

1) What was the score in the Championship Play Off Semi Final Second Leg victory over Leeds in 2019?

2) Derby hammered Nottingham Forest by what score in March 2014?

3) Derby had a promising start to the 2010/11 Championship season, including a 5-0 win over which team in September 2010?

4) Preston North End were beaten by what score at Pride Park in April 2004?

5) Who scored twice as Derby came from 2-1 down to beat Bournemouth in the Championship in November 2021?

6) Which team did Derby beat 4-0 in the Premier League in March 2000?

7) Who scored a hat-trick in the 6-1 win over Rotherham in March 2019?

8) Paul Peschisolido scored twice during a 4-2 victory over Nottingham Forest in which year?

9) Which defender scored a sensational overhead kick deep into stoppage time to secure a 2-2 draw with Birmingham City in January 2022?

10) Who scored the only goal late on in the 1-0 win over Forest in the Championship in January 2010?

Red Cards

1) Who was sent off deep into second half injury time as the Rams lost 2-1 away to Forest in January 2022?

2) Which Derby goalkeeper was sent off during the 2-1 away victory over Nottingham Forest in September 2011?

3) Chris Baird was shown a red card late on during a 3-3 draw with which team in February 2018?

4) What was unusual about the red card Tom Lawrence received against Reading in June 2020?

5) Derby held on for a point away to Crewe in September 2005 after seeing which defender dismissed in the second half?

6) Warren Barton was given his marching orders during a 2-0 home defeat to which team in a Division One clash in September 2002?

7) VAR was used to send off a player for the first time ever in a FA Cup match during the Derby clash with which Premier League side in January 2020?

8) Robbie Savage ended up playing in goal against reading in 2010 after which goalkeeper was sent off on his debut?

9) John Esutace was sent off in stoppage time as Derby claimed a 1-0 away win against which team in January 2015?

10) Who saw red during the 3-1 defeat to Chelsea in the League Cup in December 2014?

Managers

1) Who was the manager of Derby County at the beginning of the 21st century?

2) In which year did George Burley become the club's manager?

3) Who replaced Burley when he left the role?

4) Who was the club's manager when they were relegated from the Premier League in 2008?

5) Derby lost 1-0 away to which team in Nigel Clough's final game as the boss?

6) Paul Clement replaced which manager when he took over the reins in 2015?

7) For how many matches did Nigel Pearson manage the team in 2016?

8) Steve McClaren returned in 2013 and secured a 1-0 win over which team in his first game back in charge?

9) Frank Lampard led Derby to what League position in his only season as manager?

10) Wayne Rooney won only one of his first seven games as gaffer, against which team did he gain the victory?

First Goals

Can you name the club that these players scored their first goal for the club against?

1) Fabrizio Ravanelli
   Blackburn Rovers
   Bolton Wanderers
   Burnley

2) Paul Peschisolido
   Sheffield United
   Sheffield Wednesday
   Rotherham United

3) Tom Huddlestone
   Brentford
   Fulham
   Millwall

4) Steve Howard
   Birmingham City
   Wolves
   West Brom

5) Jamie Ward
   Sunderland
   Hull City
   Middlesbrough

6) Chris Martin
   Nottingham Forest
   Hull City
   Leicester City

7) Darren Bent
   Chesterfield
   Chester City
   Hull City

8) Sam Baldock
   Nottingham Forest
   Bournemouth
   Hull City

9) Ravel Morrison
   Salford City
   Sheffield United
   Birmingham City

10) Luke Plange

Blackburn Rovers
Blackpool
Bournemouth

Transfers Part Two

1) Which player signed on a free transfer from Nottingham Forest in June 2011?

2) Who was sold to Celtic in the 2011 January transfer window?

3) Stephen Bywater moved to which club after leaving Derby in 2012?

4) From which team did Derby sign Richard Keogh in 2012?

5) John Brayford was sold to which club in July 2013?

6) Who was purchased from Tottenham Hotspur in January 2014?

7) Which two players arrived from Aston Villa in June 2015?

8) Who was bought from Hull City in July 2015?

9) Ryan Shotton left Derby in July 2016 to sign for which side?

10) Who was sold to Burnley for over £10 million in August 2016?

11) From which club did Derby buy David Nugent in 2017?

12) Which goalkeeper was sold to Stoke City in January 2017?

13) Derby brought in Tom Lawrence from where in August 2017?

14) Who joined French side Guingamp on a free transfer after leaving Derby in 2017?

15) Who moved from Brentford to Derby in July 2018?

16) From which American team did Ashley Cole arrive in 2019?

17) George Thorne moved permanently to which team in January 2020?

18) Which two players moved to Sheffield United in September 2020?

19) Ravel Morrison had been playing for which side before signing for Derby in July 2021?

20) Who was sold to Wigan for a nominal fee during the 2022 winter transfer window?

Answers

General Knowledge Answers

1) Derby won their first game of the 21st century, a 2-0 win thanks to a brace from Branko Strupar against which team on the 3rd of January 2000?
Watford

2) Which company was Derby's main shirt sponsor during the 2007/08 Premier League campaign?
Derbyshire Building Society

3) Who was the club's top scorer in the 2017/18 Championship season with 21 goals?
Matej Vydra

4) Tom Huddlestone made his debut in 2003 in an opening day fixture against which team?
Stoke City

5) Which player became the first Austrian to represent the club when he signed in 2015?
   Andreas Weimann

6) Who became Derby's youngest ever goal scorer when he netted in an FA Cup victory over Tranmere in 2013 aged just 16 years and 5 months old?
   Mason Bennett

7) Which side did Derby beat on aggregate to progress to the Championship Play Off Final of 2007?
   Southampton

8) Who scored the winner in that 2007 final against West Brom?
   Stephen Pearson

9) Tom Huddlestone made his debut in 2003 in an opening day fixture against which team?
   Stoke City

10) Which squad number did Tom Ince wear during his time at the club?

23

11) Who did Robbie Savage replace as club captain in 2008?

Matt Oakley

12) Who scored a calamitous own goal late on to hand Middlesbrough a 1-1 draw at the Riverside in October 2018?

Jayden Bogle

13) England beat which county 4-0 at Pride Park in May 2001?

Mexico

14) Who scored a hat trick in the 4-2 win over Fulham in April 2017?

David Nugent

15) Ashley Cole made his final appearance as a professional in a match versus which team in April 2019?

Birmingham City

16) Who scored the winner as Derby won their only game of the 2007/08 Premier League season against Newcastle?
Kenny Miller

17) Which other two teams were relegated alongside Derby in the 2001/02 Premiership season?
Leicester City and Ipswich Town

18) Derby lost 1-0 to QPR in the 2014 Championship Play Off final despite which opposition player being dismissed with the score at 0-0?
Gary O'Neil

19) By what aggregate score line did Derby defeat Leeds in their dramatic Play Off Semi Final tie in 2019?
Derby 4-3 Leeds United

20) Derby escaped relegation on the last day of the 2020/21 Championship season by drawing with Sheffield Wednesday, but what was the final score?

Derby 3-3 Sheffield Wednesday

Transfers Part One Answers

1) From which side did Derby buy Georgi Kinkladze in April 2000?
   Ajax

2) Who was sold to Lens in June 2000?
   Esteban Fuertes

3) Which player was bought from Manchester United in July 2000?
   Danny Higginbotham

4) Dean Sturridge left to join which side in January 2001?
   Leicester City

5) Derby signed which two players from Newcastle United in February 2002?
   Warren Barton and Rob Lee

6) Which midfielder was sold to Leeds United in October 2001?
   Seth Johnson

7) Derby sold which two players to Middlesbrough in January 2003?
Chris Riggott and Malcolm Christie

8) From which club was Paul Peschisolido signed in 2004?
Sheffield United

9) Fabrizio Ravanelli joined which Scottish side on a free transfer after leaving in 2003?
Dundee

10) Inigo Idiakez signed on a free from which Spanish club in the summer of 2004?
Rayo Vallecano

11) Which centre back joined from West Brom in January 2006?
Darren Moore

12) Tom Huddlestone was sold to which Premier League team in 2005?
Tottenham Hotspur

13) From which club did Derby buy Robert Earnshaw in 2007?
Norwich City

14) Goalkeeper Roy Carroll signed on a free from which club in January 2008?
Rangers

15) Which winger arrived from Spanish side Levante in the 2008 January transfer window?
Laurent Robert

16) Which defender signed on a free in November 2008 having left Southampton?
Darren Powell

17) Who was sold to Hull City in July 2008?
Craig Fagan

18) Derby signed which two players from Burton in July 2009?
Saul Deeney and Jake Buxton

19) Which England international midfielder joined from Sheffield United in September 2009?
Lee Hendrie

20) Claude Davis joined which club after leaving Derby in September 2009?
Crystal Palace

Cup Games Answers

1) Who scored the winner in the 1-0 victory over Crystal Palace in the FA Cup Third Round in January 2020?
Chris Martin

2) What was the final score in the incredible penalty shoot-out win over Carlisle in the League Cup Second Round win in 2016?
Derby 14-13 Carlisle

3) Which non-league team knocked Derby out of the FA Cup in January 2011?
Crawley Town

4) Which team knocked The Rams out of the league cup in both 2000 and 2001?
Fulham

5) Derby lost 3-1 at home to which team in the 2014 League Cup Quarter Final?
Chelsea

6) By what score were Nottingham Forest beaten in the 2009 FA Cup Fourth Round replay at the City Ground?
Nottingham Forest 2-3 Derby County

7) Derby smashed which team 5-0 in the 2013 League Cup Second Round?
Brentford

8) Derby also won 5-0 in the FA Cup in 2013, defeating which side?
Tranmere Rovers

9) Which five teams did Derby knock out on their way to the Semi Final of the 2008/09 League Cup?
Lincoln City, Preston North End, Brighton, Leeds United and Stoke City

10) Derby won the first leg of the 2009 Semi Final, beating Manchester United 1-0 thanks to a goal from which player?
Kris Commons

Memorable Games Answers

1) What was the score in the Championship Play Off Semi Final Second Leg victory over Leeds in 2019?
Leeds United 2-4 Derby County (3-4 on aggregate)

2) Derby hammered Nottingham Forest by what score in March 2014?
Derby 5-0 Nottingham Forest

3) Derby had a promising start to the 2010/11 Championship season, including a 5-0 win over which team in September 2010?
Crystal Palace

4) Preston North End were beaten by what score at Pride Park in April 2004?
Derby 5-1 Preston

5) Who scored twice as Derby came from 2-1 down to beat Bournemouth in the Championship in November 2021?
Tom Lawrence

6) Which team did Derby beat 4-0 in the Premier League in March 2000?
Wimbledon

7) Who scored a hat-trick in the 6-1 win over Rotherham in March 2019?
Martyn Waghorn

8) Paul Peschisolido scored twice during a 4-2 victory over Nottingham Forest in which year?
2004

9) Which defender scored a sensational overhead kick deep into stoppage time to secure a 2-2 draw with Birmingham City in January 2022?
Krystian Bielik

10) Who scored the only goal late on in the 1-0 win over Forest in the Championship in January 2010?
Rob Hulse

Red Cards Answers

1) Who was sent off deep into second half injury time as the Rams lost 2-1 away to Forest in January 2022?
Ravel Morrison

2) Which Derby goalkeeper was sent off during the 2-1 away victory over Nottingham Forest in September 2011?
Frank Fielding

3) Chris Baird was shown a red card late on during a 3-3 draw with which team in February 2018?
Reading

4) What was unusual about the red card Tom Lawrence received against Reading in June 2020?
He was sent off after full-time

5) Derby held on for a point away to Crewe in September 2005 after seeing which defender dismissed in the second half?
Andrew Davies

6) Warren Barton was given his marching orders during a 2-0 home defeat to which team in a Division One clash in September 2002?
Preston North End

7) VAR was used to send off a player for the first time ever in a FA Cup match during the Derby clash with which Premier League side in January 2020?
Crystal Palace (The player was Luka Milivojevic)

8) Robbie Savage ended up playing in goal against reading in 2010 after which goalkeeper was sent off on his debut?
Saul Deeney

9) John Esutace was sent off in stoppage time as Derby claimed a 1-0 away win against which team in January 2015?
Ipswich Town

10) Who saw red during the 3-1 defeat to Chelsea in the League Cup in December 2014?
Jake Buxton

Managers Answers

1) Who was the manager of Derby County at the beginning of the 21st century?
Jim Smith

2) In which year did George Burley become the club's manager?
2003

3) Who replaced Burley when he left the role?
Phil Brown

4) Who was the club's manager when they were relegated from the Premier League in 2008?
Paul Jewell

5) Derby lost 1-0 away to which team in Nigel Clough's final game as the boss?
Nottingham Forest

6) Paul Clement replaced which manager when he took over the reins in 2015?
Steve McClaren

7) For how many matches did Nigel Pearson manage the team in 2016?
12

8) Steve McClaren returned in 2013 and secured a 1-0 win over which team in his first game back in charge?
Leeds United

9) Frank Lampard led Derby to what League position in his only season as manager?
6th

10) Wayne Rooney won only one of his first seven games as gaffer, against which team did he gain the victory?
Millwall

First Goals Answers

1) Fabrizio Ravanelli
   Blackburn Rovers

2) Paul Peschisolido
   Rotherham United

3) Tom Huddlestone
   Brentford

4) Steve Howard
   Wolves

5) Jamie Ward
   Middlesbrough

6) Chris Martin
   Leicester City

7) Darren Bent
   Chesterfield

8) Sam Baldock
   Hull City

9) Ravel Morrison
   Salford City

10) Luke Plange
   Blackpool

Transfers Part Two Answers

1) Which player signed on a free transfer from Nottingham Forest in June 2011?
Nathan Tyson

2) Who was sold to Celtic in the 2011 January transfer window?
Kris Commons

3) Stephen Bywater moved to which club after leaving Derby in 2012?
Sheffield Wednesday

4) From which team did Derby sign Richard Keogh in 2012?
Coventry City

5) John Brayford was sold to which club in July 2013?
Cardiff City

6) Who was purchased from Tottenham Hotspur in January 2014?
Simon Dawkins

7) Which two players arrived from Aston Villa in June 2015?

Darren Bent and Andreas Weimann

8) Who was bought from Hull City in July 2015?

Tom Ince

9) Ryan Shotton left Derby in July 2016 to sign for which side?

Birmingham City

10) Who was sold to Burnley for over £10 million in August 2016?

Jeff Hendrick

11) From which club did Derby buy David Nugent in 2017?

Middlesbrough

12) Which goalkeeper was sold to Stoke City in January 2017?

Lee Grant

13) Derby brought in Tom Lawrence from where in August 2017?
Leicester City

14) Who joined French side Guingamp on a free transfer after leaving Derby in 2017?
Abdoul Camara

15) Who moved from Brentford to Derby in July 2018?
Florian Jozefzoon

16) From which American team did Ashley Cole arrive in 2019?
LA Galaxy

17) George Thorne moved permanently to which team in January 2020?
Oxford United

18) Which two players moved to Sheffield United in September 2020?
Max Lowe and Jayden Bogle

19) Ravel Morrison had been playing for which side before signing for Derby in July 2021?
Den Haag

20) Who was sold to Wigan for a nominal fee during the 2022 winter transfer window?
Graeme Shinnie

If you enjoyed this book please consider leaving a five star review on Amazon

Books by Jack Pearson available on Amazon:

Cricket:

Cricket World Cup 2019 Quiz Book
The Ashes 2019 Cricket Quiz Book
The Ashes 2010-2019 Quiz Book
The Ashes 2005 Quiz Book
The Indian Premier League Quiz Book

Football:

The Quiz Book of Premier League Football
Transfers
The Quiz Book of the England Football
Team in the 21st Century
The Quiz Book of Arsenal Football Club in
the 21st Century
The Quiz Book of Aston Villa Football Club
in the 21st Century
The Quiz Book of Chelsea Football Club in
the 21st Century
The Quiz Book of Everton Football Club in
the 21st Century

The Quiz Book of Leeds United Football Club in the 21st Century

The Quiz Book of Leicester City Football Club in the 21st Century

The Quiz Book of Liverpool Football Club in the 21st Century

The Quiz Book of Manchester City Football Club in the 21st Century

The Quiz Book of Manchester United Football Club in the 21st Century

The Quiz Book of Newcastle United Football Club in the 21st Century

The Quiz Book of Southampton Football Club in the 21st Century

The Quiz Book of Sunderland Association Football Club in the 21st Century

The Quiz Book of Tottenham Hotspur Football Club in the 21st Century

The Quiz Book of West Ham United Football Club in the 21st Century

The Quiz Book of Wrexham Association Football Club in the 21st Century

Printed in Great Britain
by Amazon

80866120R00031